SELF-EVOLUTION

SELF-EVOLUTION

Break Free and Discover The Real You

Anthony Butto
Founder of Journey Evolution

Published by Anthony Butto, A Journey Evolution Project

Contact me:

mailto:anthony@journeyevolution.com

Copyright © 2017 by Anthony Butto

ISBN-13: 978-0692821398
ISBN-10: 0692821392

To Den and Jenny, you know the struggles I have faced, you have seen the progress I have made; and you have supported me wholeheartedly every step of the way.

Thank you!

Author's Statement

Hello. My name's Anthony Butto. Just call me Anthony.

I wrote this book to, not tell but, help people find out who they are. After all, no one could tell me who I was. They could be kind or they could be painful but they couldn't tell me who I was. So I can't tell you who you are. I can only help you find that out.

Many people feel like they don't belong. They're suffering. Until not so long ago, I was right there myself.

I acted against myself. I defeated myself. I felt lost, lonely, and disconnected. My decisions were led by those feelings, and our decisions are who we are. They are our character, and character permeates all aspects of our lives.

What I'm saying is, I was fear. I was lonely. I was disconnected.

I spent much of my life throwing away opportunities I felt I didn't deserve. I filled my life with people who didn't deserve me.

I finally decided it was time to change my life.

I remember that moment. The moment it all changed. It was like a button had been pressed, a fire lit. In that moment it was like the old Anthony had died and a new Anthony had been born to take his place.

There was only one problem. I wasn't sure who exactly this new Anthony was.

I would come to realize, this newcomer was secretly being born all the time that old self had been alive. Though he had been hidden under disappointment and pain, in that instant a new Anthony was revealed by truth. And now, that Anthony is sitting here, writing this book, discovering himself in the process. That Anthony is reaching out to you now. That Anthony is going to help you die, and, most importantly, help you be born.

Contents

Introduction

Do you feel lost, without direction or purpose? Do you lack motivation and desire?

Do you feel like you aren't good enough to have the things you want in life?

You're numb.

You're a zombie, but not in the way the zombies are on The Walking Dead, the TV show. Your skin tone is definitely much better and you don't have the craving for human flesh, at least I hope you don't.

Nonetheless, you're a zombie.

You wake up every morning still exhausted from the night before. You go to work at an unfulfilling job that leaves you drained like an old battery that has been sitting in a drawer for years. Perhaps you come home to an empty house or to someone who doesn't appreciate you. You spend countless hours on social media or watching TV. You try to escape your reality. You eat junk food or drink alcohol to ease the pain that you call "life." Then, as soon as it's over, it's time go to bed...

And, worst of all, you repeat it. You repeat it all over again the next day.

But this can't be all there is to your life.

Or is it?

You know there has to be something more. You know you deserve better. You feel it inside your very soul.

But you don't really know who you are or what you want.

You fear these are the cards that you were dealt, that you need to just accept it for what it is.

So, what do you do?

The same thing you've always done.

Nothing.

Maybe it's time to throw those old cards back at the dealer, to look him straight in the eye, and demand new ones.

But you're afraid. You're scared.

It's time you gain a better understanding of who you are, what it is you want, why you really want it, and how you can start working towards achieving it.

It's time you start taking action in all of those areas of your life that are crying out for change, either emotionally, mentally, physically, or financially.

Just think. If you are unhappy with your life now, how will it be five years from now? Ten years from now? Or even one year from now if you don't take action today?

Do you still want to be stuck in the same situation you are in now?

Well you don't have to be.

"The best way to predict the future is to create it."
- Abraham Lincoln

Are you ready?

Phase One

The Discovery: Who are you?

> *"If you don't know who you truly are, you'll never know what you really want."*
>
> **— Roy T. Bennett**

Who are you?

Do you know?

If someone asked you right now to tell them about yourself, what would you say?

In this phase, we will take a closer look at who you are.

Passion Within

Passion is defined as the strong feeling of enthusiasm or excitement for something.

One aspect of knowing who you really are is to discover your passion.

What are your passions? What gives you a sense of enthusiasm? What excites you?

> *"Anything that gets your blood racing is probably worth doing."*
> **— Hunter S. Thompson**

Nowadays with social media, the internet, TV, video games, etc., our attention gets devoured by multiple sources at any given time. We lose focus on the things that are most meaningful and fulfilling to us, while looking for that "quick fix." Yet it is these shortcuts that lead to a short-lived feeling of satisfaction which leaves us empty in the long term.

When I started looking within myself, I realized that what I thought were passions of mine actually turned out to be what I call Reality Blinders. I define reality blinders as things we do to pass the time that don't add any value or substance to our lives. They provide a kind of satisfaction that eventually fades away.

I used to spend countless hours binge watching every episode of TV shows like Breaking Bad and Dexter. Don't get me wrong, each had some amazing story-telling.

But what guess happened at the end of finishing each?

SPOILER ALERT

I was annoyed, frustrated, unfulfilled. My life had not changed, had not improved. Plus, to find out after all of that, Heisenberg dies and Dexter becomes a fucking lumberjack...

There were also the video games...

There were some weekends where I wouldn't even leave my house because I was trying to level a virtual character or beat a certain stage. I had to upgrade that laser cannon in order to destroy the hordes of monsters attacking everything in sight! I had to keep playing until I reached that save point! I had to defeat the evil warlord before he conquered the planet! The fate of the Universe depended on it! Were those my true passions because I devoted most of my free time to them?

No.

> *"Don't waste your time chasing things that will never be beneficial to your future."*
> *— April Mae Monterrosa*

I had to push those *reality blinders* off to the side, as if they were the bag of Halloween candy I refused to let go of after a long night of trick or treating as a child, in order to look deeper within myself and recognize my passions.

I discovered that it's the time I spend learning a new Maroon 5 or Paramore song on my guitar. It's the hours creating a new computer animation like the dancing alien or rapping M&M (which are actually still on YouTube somewhere). It's the 60-90 minutes working out in the gym each morning listening to dance/club music. Or, more recently, the 30 minutes I spend reading each night before going to bed. These are my true passions. These are the things that excite me and give me a strong sense of fulfillment.

It wasn't until I started devoting less time to my reality blinders and more time to my passions, that I start having more enthusiasm and a sense of fulfillment on a day-to-day basis. I had a better feeling about myself and who I was.

> *"Renew your passions daily."*
> — *Terri Guillemets*

Most people choose to spend a lot of their free time doing things they think will give them joy or excitement (TV, social media, video games, porn). However, in most instances, these things leave you feeling worse than you did before you engaged in them.

The reason I call them reality binders is that they keep you from exploring and discovering your true passions. It's only your true passions that give you a better sense of who you are.

> "Chase down your passion like it's the last bus of the night."
> — *Terri Guillemets*

So let's start discovering your passions. Here are a few questions to help get you thinking:

- What do you enjoy doing that doesn't feel like work?

- What is something you could spend hours doing that makes you feel alive?

- If you had 60 minutes of free time each day, how would you spend it?

Avoid these common mistakes:

- Mistaking a reality blinder as a true passion
- Thinking you don't have any passions

> "A life without passion is not living, it's merely existing."
> — *Leo Buscaglia*

You need start sorting through your reality blinders and true passions. Don't let weeks, months, or even years, pass you by without knowing your passion within.

Take action right now. Take a piece of paper. Think back to practices and activities that you've left behind but have always promised yourself to return to. It could be things you've stopped doing entirely. It could be things that you don't do enough of. It could even be things you've always wanted to try.

The answer is not always black and white. What we want to do is to see our reality binders and passions clearly. So write out all of your reality blinders in one column and all of your true passions in another column.

Super Powers

To define the term *super powers*, let's use the example of one of my favorite superheroes growing up as a kid, and even to this day, Superman. Superman has heat vision, superhuman strength, the ability to fly, X-ray vision, and super hearing just to name a few.

Hopefully, you can see that by using Superman as an example I am referring to the term super powers as one's strengths.

Another aspect of knowing who you really are is to discover your super powers.

What are your super powers? What are your strengths? What are you good at?

> *"No one can discover you until you do. Exploit your talents, skills and strengths and make the world sit up and take notice."*
> **– Rob Liano**

We don't often take the time to acknowledge our super powers a.k.a. our strengths. We tend to focus only on the negative side of things. In doing so, our strengths become ignored. We lose sight of what they are.

Imagine if Superman ignored all of his strengths and abilities and focused only on the negative side effects kryptonite immediately has on him when in his presence. (For those of you who aren't familiar with kryptonite, it's a radioactive element from Superman's home planet of Krypton which weakens him.)

If Superman had that defeatist mindset, would he still want to save people or stop the bad guys knowing kryptonite could potentially show up along the way at any moment? No, probably not. He would have lost sight of all the amazing things he can do.

This goes for everyone, including myself. How could I expect to have the motivation or drive to do anything when my constant negative thinking was like a Gatling gun of armor piercing bullets to my confidence?

I thought I wasn't smart enough to go for that promotion.

I thought I wasn't man enough to keep that relationship together.

I thought I wasn't strong enough to push my weights in the gym.

> *"Don't let a weakness make you weak."*
> **— Aimee Cohen**

I had to shift that negative outlook in order to recognize and acknowledge my strengths. I had to stop ignoring that I am a good listener, that I am disciplined, that I am a quick learner, that I am enthusiastic. I can definitely add more of my strengths but I think you get the idea. The main goal here is to focus on your strengths. Avoid focusing on the negative.

Most people focus only on their negative thoughts because they don't feel that they have strengths or at least not many.

I think everyone has an arsenal of super powers at their disposal. We need to just take the time to discover what those are. It's those strengths that can help us push through those negative thoughts that may be holding us back.

> *"What is my strength? Do I even have a strength? Maybe I have too many strengths, and that's why I can't think of just one."*
> **— Wendy Mass,** *Jeremy Fink and the Meaning of Life*

Let's start discovering your super powers. Here are a few ways to help you get thinking:

- Send your negative thinking on a permanent vacation
- Realize everyone has strengths, including you
- Acknowledge your positive qualities

Avoid these common mistakes:

- Overlooking a hidden strength
- Thinking a quality beneficial to you or others is not a strength

An example could be you are good at making people laugh... That's a fuckin' super power!!

> *"Being funny is one of my greatest strengths. I can make girls smile when they're down, and when they're having a good time, I can carry on the joke."*
> **— John Krasinski**

You need start discovering your strengths now. It's important to bust through your negative thoughts, unlock your strengths, and start taking advantage of them.

So this is what we'll do. We'll make a list. Take some time to sit down and think of all your character traits, your knowledge, your experience and just write them down. These can be little things. These can be big things. They can be things that other people don't appreciate.

Whatever they may be, write them down. I think when you see your strengths in front of you, you'll start to realize how strong you really are. Explore your strengths and write them down before continuing.

Triumphs

Triumph is defined as a significant success or noteworthy achievement; an instance or occasion of victory.

Discovering your triumphs is another ingredient of knowing who you really are. They let you know what you consider to be a success, and that they're worth reaching for.

So what are your accomplishments? What are your successes? What struggles have you overcome in life?

> *"The triumph can't be had without the struggle."*
> **- Wilma Rudolph**

We often forget the importance of our past experiences or struggles. Our ability to overcome obstacles in life is just as important in discovering who we are as our future endeavors. It's those triumphs along the way, big or small, that help shape us into stronger individuals. They could include getting through a tough breakup or divorce, running a marathon, giving a presentation at work, becoming a parent, finishing school, or starting a business. Hopefully, you can easily start to see that our lives are filled with triumphs, and we need to recognize their significance.

Looking back, there are plenty of moments I can think of that I am proud of. We all have them. One of my most recent triumphs was going on my first solo trip and dealing with my social anxiety head on. I've always had trouble in social settings, especially where I didn't know many people. If you are personally familiar with social anxiety, or know someone dealing with it, you know being around a bunch of strangers for any extended period of time is not typically a situation we thrive in.

So, in September of 2016, I decided to go to Universal Studios Orlando for a week by myself. Talk about jumping straight in to the fire, right? There is no way to avoid people there. Yet I love the thrill rides, the Halloween event at Universal is always awesome, and I had vacation time off from work.

I remember the morning I was getting ready to head out to the airport. I looked down at my Fitbit. My heartrate was higher than when Indiana Jones was being chased by angry natives after stealing the sacred golden head from the cave of death in Raiders of the Lost Ark.

> *"There are no negatives in life, only challenges to overcome that will make you stronger."*
> **- Eric Bates**

At the beginning of the trip, I was pretty much a nervous wreck. As the trip continued on, I slowly became more comfortable meeting and conversing with people along the way. By the end of the trip, I had met so many interesting people, enjoyed some great experiences, and I just didn't want to leave.

Being able to face my social anxiety in this way was a definite triumph. Although my social anxiety will still sneak up on me from time to time, I overcame that situation. It was a major accomplishment and has made me stronger.

> *"A great accomplishment shouldn't be the end of the road, just the starting point for the next leap forward."*
> *- Harvey Mackay*

Most people don't view their triumphs as being major factors in the development of their character.

I see the ability to overcome a struggle, big or small, whether it was yesterday, a month ago, or five years ago, and to be here today to talk about it, as a triumph that has helped shape who you are.

> *"The greatest accomplishment is not in never falling, but in rising again after you fall."*
> *- Vince Lombardi*

So let's start discovering your triumphs. Look back at your past and ask yourself:

- What struggles, if any, have you overcome?
- How did those moments make you feel after you got through them?
- How did that change you moving forward?

Avoid these common mistakes:

- Thinking a negative past experience is not a triumph
- Thinking your accomplishments don't shape who you are

"The harder the conflict, the more glorious the triumph."
- Thomas Paine

You can't discover your triumphs if you don't know what led to them. Use the past as your guide. It is important to remember the pain or hardship of a past experience, how it truly felt at the time. Focus on how it helped you move beyond it and toward who you are today.

Take action right now. Take a paper and pen and write down all of the triumphs in your life that you can think of. You can always return and write more down if you remember other triumphs later.

Role Models

A *Role Model* is defined as a person who enjoys wide recognition for their excellence of character and/or ability. They are often eagerly admired by people who pursue the same values, goals or behavior.

Discovering your role models is another factor toward finding out who you are. Knowing who you admire can allow you to understand what it is you value, and even why or how you might want to emulate your role model's success.

As before, we must ask ourselves who are our role models? Who do we admire? Who do we respect greatly?

> *"The role that people play in your life can determine how far you can go."*
> *- Israelmore Ayivor*

Most of us have had someone we've looked up to, either in our own life or in the public eye. Looking at those we admire, we see in them the qualities or characteristics we would also like to have in our arsenal of super powers. Our role models show us who we aspire to become. By looking at our role models closely, they can inspire and motivate us to become stronger individuals.

However, there are times we may view our role models with feelings of jealousy or envy. These negative feelings can discourage in abandoning our comfort zones and acquiring any motivation to change.

I've had plenty of role models, in my life and in the public eye. Each of them had a quality or qualities I admired. But to be honest, for the longest time I viewed my role models with feelings of jealousy and envy. I often thought "I wish I could be more like that", but I didn't take the opportunity to learn from them. I didn't allow myself to use my role models as a source of motivation and drive to become better.

Instead of learning that crazy guitar solo from one of my favorite guitar players, Nuno Bettencourt from the band Extreme, I thought "Oh snap! That was amazing! There is absolutely no way I can do that." And I never attempted to learn or practice the technique to be able to play it. I had already labeled it as something that would be out of my reach forever. I had prescribed myself a limit.

I can find another example in a friend of mine, who is comfortable in any situation and might bust out with that perfect witty phrase at the perfect moment. I would think "Ugh, how the heck does he do that?" My witty phrases usually came two days after the situation had passed, sometime while I was trying to fall asleep at night. Unfortunately, a warm pillow is not a good listener of wit.

> *"Transform jealousy to admiration, and what you admire will become part of your life."*
> **— Yoko Ono**

Changing my perception of my role models from a view of jealousy and envy toward an appreciation of what I admired about them, allowed me to learn from my role models. It allowed me to move towards improving myself.

I can now focus more on their positive attributes and take action to become a stronger person.

> *"I think a role model is a mentor - someone you see on a daily basis, and you learn from them."*
> **— Denzel Washington**

Most people think their role models have to be someone famous, or that their role models are people that we could only resemble in fantasy.

However, I see a role model as being anyone who has qualities I respect and admire. Don't limit yourself to a public figure or TV star. Look around yourself. Allow your role models to inspire you to your own greatness.

> *"Pick you role models wisely, find out what they did and do it."*
> **— Lana Del Ray**

17

Let's start discovering your role models. Begin to ask the following questions:

- Who are your role models?
- Why do you respect them?
- What can you learn from them?

Avoid these common mistakes:

- Thinking about your role models with feelings of jealousy and envy
- Not using your role models as motivation to improve yourself

---

"Work until your idols become your rivals."
— Drake

Use your role models as motivation. Discover who it is you want to strive towards becoming.

Let's add to that list again. Take a new heading and think about all of the people you've ever admired. Include those you had as a child, those you have as an adult. It can be interesting to see how our ideas on what is to be admired change as we get older.

Sometimes the thing we admire in a childhood role model is the same thing we love and respect in a later one. So remember to jot down why you see or saw them as a role model as well. You'll learn about yourself doing this. I promise.

Diamonds

In the literal sense, a *diamond* is defined as a transparent, flawless, or almost flawless, piece of stone, especially when cut and polished, and valued as a precious gem.

When you think of diamonds, what comes to mind?

Imagine you have a handful of diamonds right now. Would you care for them? Keep them safe? Cherish them? Display them? Take pride in them? Perhaps show them off because you are proud of them?

Now imagine the above scenario again. Replace that handful of diamonds with your core values. Would you take care of them in the same way? Would you find them equally as important and precious?

Another vital component of knowing who you really are is to discover your diamonds.

What are your diamonds? What are your core values? What do you stand for?

> *"Living in a way that reflects one's values is not just about what you do, it is also about how you do things."*
> — **Deborah Day**

Your diamonds a.k.a. your core values, are the beliefs, principles, or ideas that are important to you.

They are the framework of your life. They define who you are and how you go about being you. They exemplify what matters most to you.

Values give us a sense of purpose. They also prevent us from making poor choices.

However, if we do not live in accordance with our values, unhappiness and frustration arise.

When I started to spend time thinking about what my core values were, so much started to make sense to me. For many years I was unhappy, unsatisfied, and unfulfilled with my life and my relationships. It wasn't until I realized that I was living in conflict with my values.

Two specific core values I considered most important to me were communication and honesty, but I was not living a life based on those values. I was living the complete opposite. I was out of alignment with myself. I was not a very good communicator, especially in my relationships and with my family. I often lied to my friends, my family, and even myself. Communication and honesty were on the top of my list, but I didn't hold myself accountable to them.

This was definitely the case in my last relationship. My girlfriend and I had been together for almost two years. I had been unhappy with how things were going for a number of months and I'm pretty sure she recognized it too. But I didn't communicate how I was feeling. I wasn't being honest with her. I kept everything locked up inside. I wasn't living the way I wanted to live. It wasn't fair to me or to my girlfriend.

And after keeping my feelings bottled up for so long, anger and resentment started setting in. Guess what happens when you start shaking that bottle and the pressure builds up over time? It creates a mess!

My relationship ended that night. The night I finally exploded under the pressure.

> *"Never compromise your values."*
> **— Steve Maraboli**

If I had lived by my core values from the beginning, who knows if we would still be together today. I don't know if we would have been able to work out our issues, but I know that if I had held myself accountable to what I believed in, we both would have been in a better state to deal with it.

It was that situation that led me to realign with my values. I am now more aware and focused on living my life in accordance with what I believe in, and it's helped provide more clarity as to who I really am.

> *"Values aren't buses... They're not supposed to get you anywhere. They're supposed to define who you are."*
> **— Jennifer Crusie**

21

Most people are out of alignment with their values, holding others accountable to those values but not themselves.

I see values as a vital aspect of defining who you are. Being aware and living by these important factors, they can bring you purpose, direction, and happiness to your life.

> *"When your values are clear to you, making decisions becomes easier."*
> **— Roy E. Disney**

Let's start discovering your diamonds. Here are a few steps to start the process:

- Determine what values are most meaningful to you
- Prioritize each by a level of importance
- Ask yourself if you are living in alignment with those values

Avoid these common mistakes:

- Confusing a core value vs. something that you value (ex. Money is valuable but it does not define who you are.)
- Trying to define values as goals. Values are the ideas you deem to be of great worth and give you structure. Goals are specific actions.

> *"We are all born as empty vessels which can be shaped by moral values."*
>
> *- Jerry Springer*

It's critical that you start discovering what your core values are now because if you are currently living out of alignment with any of them you will continue to have inner conflict. Your core values will give you a better sense of who you really are.

So put down the book and draw up another list. Write down your values, your diamonds, and be honest. Putting things in perspective can only work if you are honest with yourself. Ask yourself what do your values mean to you – what are you willing to part with? What can you not bear to part with?

Phase One

The Discovery: Summary

Take an inventory of what you've learned in Phase One – The Discovery.

All of those lists we've been hard at work making will now come in useful, since we're about to make, what I like to call, a Personal Discovery Statement. We'll build upon this as we go. It should look something like this:

My name is (insert your name). My passions are (insert your passions). I'm (insert your super powers). I've been able to (insert your triumphs). I'm striving to be (insert your models' qualities). I value (insert your diamonds).

Congratulations! You've made it through Phase One.

Are you ready for Phase Two?

Phase Two

The Surface: What do you want?

> "If you don't know what you want, you end up with a lot you don't."
>
> — **Chuck Palahniuk**

So now you know who you are.

But do you know what you want?

If someone asked you, "What do you want?" What would you say?

In this phase, we will take a closer look at what you want.

Self-Indulgence

elf-Indulgence is defined as indulging one's own desires, passions, whims, etc., especially without restraint.

In other words, it is the desiring you.

It may sound bold, but to start scratching the surface of knowing what you want, you need to be selfish.

So what do you want? Is it based on you or based on what others want?

> *"Sometimes you have to be selfish to be selfless."*
> **— Edward Albert**

Let me start out by justifying what I mean. Being considered "selfish" gets a bad rap. For some people reading this right now, it does not sit well with them. Yes, being selfish is about helping yourself, but it's also about taking care of any pain and heartache within you. It's about taking care of yourself. Your needs and priorities.

For those still struggling with the importance of being selfish, let's take a quick look at the Airplane Oxygen Mask Theory.

I'm sure most of us have been on an airplane. If so, you've heard the flight attendants go over the safety instructions prior to take off:

- Emergency exits are located on the right, left, and rear of the plane.
- Seat cushions may be used as floatation devices.
- In the event the air pressure drops in the cabin, put the oxygen mask on yourself before others.

In other words, if you can't help yourself, how will you be able to help the people around you?

This same theory applies to life.

You can't figure out exactly what you want if you're constantly sacrificing yourself for everyone else. You have to put yourself first because, chances are, if you don't, then no one else will.

I was always a people pleaser. I put others' happiness before my own. I would throw my happiness off to the side because I saw selfishness as a bad thing. It was a quality I didn't want to have and it was something I hated in others. The problem was that trying to make everyone happy led to me being unhappy. I had no direction. This caused me to follow everyone else's lead. I didn't really know what I wanted in life, let alone what I wanted to do over the coming weekend.

When someone asked me "What do you want to do?" or "What do want to eat?" They didn't want to hear me say "I don't know," or "Whatever you want."

Would you agree that those kinds of responses can be more annoying to hear than something you don't agree with? An indecisiveness.

See, the funny thing about selfishness is you don't realize how beneficial it can be to your soul, your life, and your relationships until you've tried it.

I'm not suggesting you become this narcissistic bastard that doesn't care about anyone but themselves. Perhaps I can sum it up with the following quote:

> "*I want you to be really, really selfish. The more selfish and nurturing you can be for yourself, the by-product for those that you love or work that you do is greatly enhanced.*"
> **– Greg Gumucio**

Once I discovered who I was, I had to learn how to be a little more selfish than I had been in the past. It has definitely helped me gain more clarity on what it is I want, not only in life but in general. It has made it easier when making decisions, helped me to establish healthy boundaries, and helped me create some concrete goals that are aligned with my core values.

> "*You can't take care of anyone else unless you first take care of yourself.*"
> **– Michael Hyatt**

Most people view selfishness as evil. They don't think of this characteristic as having positive attributes.

I view selfishness as an important characteristic in your self-nurture and personal development. It can give you direction and purpose when you are feeling lost or disconnected.

> *"Don't sacrifice yourself too much, because if you sacrifice too much there's nothing else you can give and nobody will care for you."*
> **— Karl Lagerfeld**

Let's allow your selfishness to breathe a little so you can have more clarity on what you want. Here are a few questions to help get you started:

- Are you constantly saying yes to everyone?
- Are you not making time for yourself?
- Are you choosing what you want for yourself or to please others?

Avoid these common mistakes:

- Thinking it's ok to push aside family obligations and responsibilities
- Thinking it's ok to start demanding everything from everyone

> *"Make yourself a priority in your life. After all, it's your life."*
> **— Akiroq Brost**

Start listing out some ways in which you can begin taking advantage of the selfish you. It can be helpful to think about what you've lost out on by not being selfish enough, by not asserting yourself. A rainy day, a lost opportunity.

All those times you've looked back after bearing that little spark of annoyance or disappointment until it burned over and you thought that you should have said something or done something at the time. Everyone has those moments. The words will pour if you let them.

Genie in the Lamp

G *enie* is defined as a spirit, often appearing in human form, that when summoned by a person carries out the wishes of the summoner.

To get closer to what you really want you need to unleash your genie.

We've all heard the stories about the genie in the lamp, right?

What if you had your own genie in the lamp, one who could make all of your dreams come true?

What do you dream of having? What would you wish for?

> *"When you cease to dream, you cease to live."*
> — *Malcolm Forbes*

This is the perfect opportunity to open your imagination. Let it run free.

People don't take the time to explore an idea like this. We get so caught up in our daily struggles and challenges that we think "Why bother? It's only going to make me upset thinking about the things I want but don't have." Well, what if doing this actually does the opposite? What if doing this sparks a drive in you that wasn't there before?

I, too, had that "Why bother?" mindset. I rarely tapped into my genie in the lamp. My self-limiting beliefs prevented me from doing so. It was Labor Day weekend and I decided to tag along to Atlantic City with family. We stayed at the Borgata which is my dad's preferred place to stay when there. I remember after we pulled in to valet, unpacked the car and started heading into the hotel, I spotted this red Ferrari 488 GTB sitting off to the side. It was absolutely gorgeous! I said to myself "Oh, I wish I had a car like that." For that split second I had let my genie out. I immediately shoved him back in that lamp. What do you think I said?

"I can never have a car like that. What am I thinking?"

My self-limiting beliefs prevented me from letting my imagination dream big. I wasn't able to figure out what I wanted in life and go after it because I didn't allow my wishes to spark that inner drive.

> "The future belongs to those who believe in the beauty of their dreams."
> — Eleanor Roosevelt

Now, instead of saying "Why bother?" I say "Why not?" I let my genie out of the lamp often. Case in point, here I am writing this book. Something I never thought I could do. You can't strive for something if you don't allow yourself to dream about it. Oh, and I didn't forget about you, red Ferrari...

> *"So many of our dreams at first seem impossible, then they seem improbable, and then, when we summon the will, they soon become inevitable."*
> **— Christopher Reeve**

Most people view this as a silly and pointless exercise. They have that "Fantasy will never equal Reality" mindset.

I view it as a powerful motivation tool in helping to discover what you want. You can't move towards making changes in your life if you won't allow yourself to think beyond your self-imposed limits.

> *"The possibility of the dream gives strength."*
> **— Lailah Gifty Akita**

Let's unleash your genie in the lamp. To help you get started, finish the following statements:

- I wish I had _____
- I wish I was _____
- I wish I did _____

Avoid these common mistakes:

- Limiting yourself instead of dreaming big

- Not being selfish with your genie (revisit Self-Indulgence if needed)

> *"What's the purpose of living if you don't go after your dreams?"*
> — **Samson Reiny**

Take action right now. Let your genie out of its lamp and have that conversation with it you've been fearing to. As always, list down your discoveries. We're getting closer and closer to knowing what you want.

Escapes

E_scape_ is defined as a slipping or getting away, as from confinement or restraint; to gain or regain liberty: _to escape from jail._

What is the difference between those convicts that stay stuck in jail versus those convicts that escape?

Are they smarter? Faster? Stronger? Maybe.

I believe it's their ability to know what they don't want (i.e. to be locked up) that ignites their inner desire to go after what it is they do want (i.e. to be free). Their motivation and drive becomes so strong, they refuse to settle and are willing to take their chances to escape at any cost.

I'm not advocating anyone in jail now try and break out, merely using it as an example.

Now think of this example and apply it to your life.

Go deeper. Dive past your surface toward what you want, toward what you need. Come to know your escape. Is there anything you want to escape from? What don't you want?

> "I do not always know what I want, but I do know what I don't want."
> — **Stanley Kubrick**

To get even further through the surface of knowing what you want you need to recognize your escapes.

One of the best ways when trying to figure out what you want in your life is by asking yourself what it is you don't want. This can actually be pretty easy for most because what we don't want or are trying to escape from is usually something we are dealing with currently in our lives. Think about what upsets you. It is important to be specific.

When you start pushing back on the things you don't want, what you want can really start coming in to focus.

I remember after graduating college in Connecticut, I moved back home to where I grew up in Long Island. After being on my own for several years, now moving back in my parents' house was a shock to my system. I think I was there no more than a month before I knew that living at home any longer than I needed was something I did not want! I realized I wanted to be back in Connecticut.

I managed to move back there but I needed a job fast in order to avoid moving back home. So, one of the first jobs I applied for was what was described as a "sales" job. What I didn't know was later that day I would be out walking in the pouring rain with these two other guys, going door-to-door between local businesses in downtown Hartford, trying to sell cheap knife sets and digital clocks that looked like little computers. It certainly didn't take me long to know 100 percent I did not want to do that. Ever again! And in case you're wondering... No, I didn't sell anything that day.

> "The first step to living the life that you want is leaving the life that you don't want."
> — **Unknown**

You can see in these two scenarios how acknowledging what I didn't want helped create more clarity and provide a stronger desire for what it was I did want. When you take the time to really look at what you don't want in life, whether it's at this very moment in time or something from the past, you are less likely to get stuck in a situation you might just settle for. Sadly, settling for something you don't want is a fast track to unhappiness.

Over the years, I lost track of that. I actually did end up getting stuck. I settled in many aspects of my life. These days, since I started using this technique again, I am now more focused on what it is I want to achieve.

> "So many of us have settled for what is, rather than what could be."
> — *Michael Hyatt*

Most people view what they don't want in their current lives as something and somewhere along the lines of "it is what it is." They accept those things. They settle for how things are instead of using those conditions as a bridge toward how they want their lives to be.

I view it as adding that extra fuel to the fire of your motivation and desire to make positive changes.

> *"The hardest part of changing things is knowing how much needs changing."*
> — *Martina Boone*

Let's list your escapes. Ask yourself the following questions to get started:

- What upsets you?
- What causes you unhappiness or pain?
- Are you settling with an aspect in your life? If so, with what?

Avoid these common mistakes:

- Not being honest with yourself
- Not acknowledging what you are currently settling for as an escape

> *"Happy people can look back and say they chose their life, not settled for it."*
> — *Shannon L. Alder*

Like those soldiers stuck in a prisoner of war camp, start thinking about your own Great Escape. List those escapes down!

Phase Two

The Surface: Summary

Now you have a better sense of who you are from Phase One, it's time to take an inventory of everything you've learned in Phase Two – The Surface.

Add to your Personal Discovery Statement the following:

I take care of myself by (insert your self-indulgences). I want (insert your dreams and wishes). I know I do not want (insert your escapes).

Congratulations! You've made it through Phase Two.

Let's move on.

Phase Three

The Truth: Why do you want it?

> "The end (goal) of art is to figure the hidden meaning of things and not their appearance; for in this profound truth lies their true reality, which does not appear in their external outlines."
>
> **— Joseph Conrad**

You know who you are.

You know what you want.

But do you know why it is you really want it?

If someone asked you why, what would you say?

In this phase, we will take a closer look at the underlying reasons. The why of your wants.

Symbols

A *symbol* is defined as something used for or regarded as representing something else; an image representing something else, often something immaterial; emblem, token, or sign.

Think back to when you were in school.

You're about to find out your grade from that big test in Mr. Applebee's class, you know, the test you studied (or didn't study) for the past few weeks.

You're so nervous right now. He's starting to hand back the tests and you really want that A (or C, I don't want to discriminate).

You start thinking about what that grade means to you. It could be something of great achievement or it could be the relief of knowing you don't have to repeat another year with Mr. Applebee because he smelled like liver and onions.

Whatever it is to you, that grade also had another meaning.

To start seeing the truth of why you want what you want, you need to recognize what it symbolizes.

What does each item on your wish list symbolize? What do they represent?

> *"Everything is a symbol of something, it seems, until proven otherwise."*
> **— Thomas C. Foster**

Like the Ferrari I discussed earlier, what we want in life represents something deeper. How often do you say you want some external thing or look at what others have and wish you had that too? What is it about those things that we want? We don't take the time to see what they symbolize to us. If you want something but don't know the reason you want it, how can you ever figure out what changes are needed in your life to achieve it?

When I began looking at my wish list, it took me a while to start recognizing what each thing on my list represented. What first appeared to me was a bunch of unattainable things. That Ferrari I gazed upon in Atlantic City was a smoking hot car. But was it just a car?

As I looked closer as to why I wanted that Ferrari, I realized, to me, it symbolized financial freedom and sex appeal. It was more than just a car. It was a symptom, a symbol, of success.

Let's look at this another way. If I think about the reason why I want to be physically fit, striving to look like Rocky in Rocky 4, you know that scene when he is training in Russia, lifting the logs and running in the snow? Not only was it an example of great physical condition, it symbolized confidence and toughness.

> *"It began in images and it ended in symbolism."*
>
> **— B. W. Powe**

When you want to make changes in your life, going about it in broad generalities will only lead to confusion. It was one thing for me to say I wanted something, but it was also very important to know the reason why (what was behind the symbol). I knew that finding out what it actually represented gave me even more focus and direction on the path I needed to travel towards it.

> *"If you change the way you look at things, the things you look at change."*
>
> **— Dr. Wayne Dyer**

Most people view what they want as simply that. "I want a new car. I want a different job." They don't look past that surface to decipher what those things symbolize for them.

I view trying to decipher why you want something as a way to get a better understanding of what it is you really want in life. In turn you will also determine the best course action for change.

> *"All meanings, we know, depend on the key of interpretation."*
> **— George Eliot**

Let's decipher the hidden symbols of your wants. Look the wish list you created in Phase 2 and begin to define their symbols. To help you get started, here are a few examples:

- To be in shape = Confidence
- A bigger house = Security
- A relationship = Companionship

(These are just examples. The important point is to be honest with yourself as to what your wish list symbolizes.)

Avoid these common mistakes:

- Not thinking something has a symbol (thinking too much about the surface)
- Thinking there is only one symbol when there may be more than one (one symbol can represent many things, but one thing can have many symbols)

> "There is a powerful need for symbolism, and that means the architecture must have something that appeals to the human heart."
> — Kenzo Tange

So, knowing the items on our list may be symbols for deeper themes, it's time to look beneath those items. Consider those items on your list to be masks. You must discover the faces beneath them. Take off their masks and reveal for yourself what's beneath them.

Pulling Up the Roots

R*oot* is defined as the part of a plant that develops, typically, from the radicle and grows downward into the soil, anchoring the plant and absorbing nutriment and moisture.

It's also defined as the fundamental or essential part; the source or origin of a thing.

If you've ever gone outside after any hurricane or major weather event, you have most likely seen some uprooted trees. Take a look at those roots. Think about how deep they must have grown into the earth. Just like those roots, our behaviors are anchored and structured by hidden meanings. And it is our roots that answer the important question "Why?"

To dig deep down into the truth of why you want what you want, you need to examine your roots.

What is the root of your symbols? What is their true meaning?

> *"The truth will set you free, but first it will piss you off."*
> **— Joe Klaas,** *Twelve Steps to Happiness*

Getting to the root or the true meaning of why we want something can be a very scary thing. When the truth comes out, there is no more hiding. You have to be vulnerable with yourself. Vulnerability is something most people are not used to or comfortable with.

This was a real eye opener for me! Let me expand on the symbols I talked about in the previous section by explaining their meaning to me:

Ferrari = Financial freedom:

I think a lot of people can relate to this one. To me, this meant being free of the worries of not having enough money to pay your bills or to travel wherever you wanted, whenever you wanted. To enjoy the finer things in life.

Ferrari = Sex appeal:

More sex appeal meant being able to attract any woman I wanted. You know... The "Brad Pitt Effect." The thing is, the only person that looks like Brad Pitt... is Brad Pitt! I'm just using Brad Pitt as an example, of course, but I'm sure you get the idea.

(Brad you are awesome! I love your movies! Don't sue me.)

Rocky in Russia = Confidence:

I never felt like I was enough... Never good enough, never smart enough, never strong enough. I wanted to have more confidence about being me.

Rocky in Russia = Toughness:

I wanted to be able to take on life's challenges, mental, emotional, and physical.

I remember being told by one of my ex-girlfriend's to "Man up!" That was such a bullshit line. But we can get into all of that another time. Maybe in my next book.

> *"The truth is rarely pure and never simple."*
> — **Oscar Wilde,** *The Importance of Being Earnest*

As you can see, I needed to get pretty vulnerable with myself in order to get to the true meaning of each of my symbols. Once I was able to see the truth, it helped me better understand why I wanted what I wanted.

> *"The unexamined life is not worth living."*
> — **Socrates**

Most people don't want to know the true meanings of why it is they want something. It means they will have to look within themselves, and they might not like what they see.

The truth is, finding the true meaning of what it is you want is one of the most important factors in uncovering what may be causing you pain or suffering. If you don't know what that thing you want means, how can you truly heal from within?

> *"Better a cruel truth than a comfortable delusion."*
> **— Edward Abbey**

Let's dig up the roots of your symbols and find out their meaning. To do this, start adding the meanings next to each entry on your list. We should expand on the examples from the previous section:

- To be in shape = Confidence = To believe that I am enough
- A bigger house = Security = Knowing my family is safe
- A relationship = Companionship = Having someone I can share life's experience with

Avoid these common mistakes:

- Not digging deep enough to see the true meaning of your symbols
- Being afraid to see what the true meanings are

> *"If you do not tell the truth about yourself you cannot tell it about other people."*
> **— Virginia Woolf**

By now, you can probably guess what we're going to be doing. That's right. It's time to list the symbols in your life. Think back across your life, about what the most important or effecting things in your life have been. Think about what they looked like on the surface. Think about what they truly meant.

You might find one symbol repeated in various contexts or you might find one meaning hiding beneath many different symbols. You're uprooting the personal culture of your individuality. This is the mythology of your own life. This list is a museum exhibition of those vital themes. So put those meanings behind glass for your own private exhibition of yourself.

Swallow the Pill

Acceptance is defined as the act of taking or receiving something offered. A favorable reception; approval; favor.

Now that you know the truth of why you want what you want, you need to accept that truth.

Are you able to swallow that pill? Can you accept your own truth?

> "The most terrifying thing is to accept oneself completely."
> — C.G. Jung

Accepting the truth about yourself can be a hard pill to swallow. Think of Neo in the movie, The Matrix. After he discovered the truth, he freaked out and started vomiting everywhere. It wasn't until he accepted the truth that he was able to become a kung-fu fighting, trench coat wearing, flying badass!

I'm not suggesting you will experience any episodes of vomiting, or that you'll learn kung-fu in less than five minutes for that matter. What I am saying is that by being able to accept the truth, you now have a laser focus on what you want in your life, why you want it, and you are free to achieve it.

Anthony Butto

No matter what you want and why you want it, whether it's to accomplish your goals or achieve your dreams, you must accept yourself first.

After I uncovered the truth about myself, I felt, to be honest, pretty shitty. I lost sight of all of my super powers and began focusing only on my weaknesses. I became Superman, only weighed down by kryptonite.

I began thinking of myself as only a shell of a man who lacked confidence, sex appeal, wasn't good enough, and worried about financial status constantly. And those were just a few of my roots…

Have you ever seen a snake eat its prey?

For your information, snakes don't chew, they swallow their prey whole.

Like that of a snake, I knew there was no chewing on this. I was going to have to snake this pill of acceptance and it was going to be a hard one to swallow!

But just like the snake, who digests their food over a long period of time, my acceptance would be a process that allowed me to experience my thoughts, feelings, and emotions without rejection.

> "We are at our most powerful the moment we no longer need to be powerful."
> — Eric Micha'el Leventhal

I finally did swallow that pill and accepted my truth but also made it a point to realize that I am still pretty awesome. I did this by stopping the comparison game of myself to those around me or by what society tells me how to be.

I admitted I'm not perfect and that is ok not to be perfect. I now know more about myself than ever before and I see life in a new perspective. I also continue to review my personal discovery statement often as well.

You remember the personal discovery statement you started in Phase 1, right? Go back to your notes and check it out. You are pretty awesome too!

Once we are able to accept the sum of all parts, the good and the bad, we are able to see something we can learn from. Self-acceptance doesn't mean you can't change what you don't like, it means the opposite. Self-acceptance allows you to make changes for the better.

> *"Accept yourself, your strengths, your weaknesses, your truths, and know what tools you have to fulfill your purpose."*
> **— Steve Maraboli,** *Life, the Truth, and Being Free*

Most people confuse accepting themselves as never changing, never improving, and never getting better or getting what they want in life.

By accepting myself, I am not bound by my negative thinking. I can be more open and focused on what it is exactly that I want to improve in my life.

> *"Stop trying to be less of who you are. Let this time in your life cut you open and drain all of the things that are holding you back."*
> **— Jennifer Elisabeth**

It's time to swallow the pill. Get started by asking yourself:

- How do you feel right now?
- Do you have more clarity about who you are and what you want?
- Are you able to accept both your good and your bad?

Avoid these common mistakes:

- Only focusing on your weaknesses
- Thinking you can't improve who you are

> *"No amount of self-improvement can make up for any lack of self-acceptance."*
> **— Robert Holden**

Take action right now by listing out any emotions, thoughts, or feelings you are experiencing. This is your moment to face that other you. Jekyll had his Hyde. Dr.

Frankenstein had his monster. You've got your own demons.

You might find that what you don't like about other people is a reflection of your self-criticism imposed. Remember. Dig deep. This exercise is private. No one's looking. You aren't turning up to work naked. The only person you need to be honest with is yourself. It's the most important step.

Phase Three

The Truth: Summary

It's time to take an inventory of everything you've learned in Phase Three – The Truth.

Build upon your Personal Discovery Statement by adding the following:

I want (insert your wish list) because it symbolizes (insert your symbols). I accept that the true meaning behind why I want those things is (insert your roots).

Congratulations! You've accomplished Phase Three.

You've made it this far. Don't stop now.

Phase Four

The Sacrifice: What are you willing to do to get it?

> *"It isn't sufficient just to want - you've got to ask yourself what you are going to do to get the things you want."*
>
> **— Franklin D. Roosevelt**

You know who you are.

You know what you want.

You know why you want it.

But what are you willing to do to get it?

In this phase, we will take a closer look at your willingness to go after what you want.

Time Shift

Time is defined as the system of those sequential relations that any event has to any other, as past, present, or future; indefinite and continuous duration regarded as that in which events succeed one another.

Time is a rare commodity these days. Between work, family, school, etc., how does one find the time to get anything done?

It's funny how we say we never have time but we always seem to find it for certain things, those most important to us. We use the excuse that we don't have any time when we want to avoid a certain task, person, or situation.

Are you willing to make the time to go after what you want?

> "There is never enough time to do all of the nothing we want to do."
> **— Bill Watterson**

Let me ask you, did you watch TV at all this week? Did you spend your lunch hour on the internet? Were you on social media for more than ten minutes today? Did you go to out with your friends this past weekend? Do you end up doing any random reality blinder to avoid doing something else?

When I decided I wanted to write this book, I knew that in order to get it done I needed to make the time do it. Just wanting it was not going to make the pages automatically write themselves (although that would have been a tremendous help). Using the excuse of not having any time wasn't going to work either. I had to make sacrifices and I had to be ok with it.

I had to be willing to:

- Sacrifice spending all day Sunday watching football and tracking my fantasy football team, The Diglets. Who, as I write this, are currently 6-3 and sitting in 3rd place!
- Sacrifice going to my friend's house to help him rig up the wiring to his new upstairs addition, snacking on the amazing chocolate chip cookies his wife bakes, or playing with their adorable daughter
- Sacrifice playing Call of Duty online using the big gun and calling in the chopper, even though I was pretty kickass at it

Writing this book was something I really wanted to accomplish because if I can help just one person change their life for the better, it would be worth all those sacrifices!

> *"I always make time for the things that are important to me."*
> *— Darren Criss*

I had to prioritize what was most important to me and make it happen. And sure enough, making those sacrifices, devoting the time I needed, helped me accomplish what I set out to do. I'm not going to lie. I'm not going to say it wasn't hard (especially true if you are easily distracted like myself). But if you keep reminding yourself why it is you are making these sacrifices, the battle gets easier.

> *"There's no such thing as being too busy. If you really want something, you'll make time for it."*
> **— Unknown**

Most people use the expression "there isn't enough time" as an excuse to not pursue a goal or make a life change.

I think if you want something enough you will find the time to devote to it.

> *"It is not enough to be busy. So are the ants. The question is: What are we busy about?"*
> **— Henry David Thoreau**

Let's start freeing up some time. Get started with the following steps:

- Figure out what are your biggest time wasters are

- Decide what you are willing to sacrifice to free up time to achieve what you want
- Schedule your day accordingly to devote that time towards your goal

Avoid these common mistakes:

- Thinking that anything less than an hour is not worth devoting to what you want. Make every minute count
- Coming up with excuses as to why you can't make the time to achieve a goal

> *"I'm sick of wasting time on things that don't matter."*
> — ***Alexandra Bracken,*** *The Darkest Minds*

Take action right now by listing out what you are willing to sacrifice in order to free up time to pursue your goals. Are you going to let your reality blinders stop you from going after what you really want?

Start writing!

Giving it Your All

E*ffort* is defined as the exertion of physical or mental power.

You've committed to making the time for what you want. Now, what are you going to do with that time?

I know this can be a tough one to commit to. I've given up on things multiple times. It was because I wasn't fully committed to the task at hand and when the going got tough, I gave up. I wasn't willing to give it my all. I wasn't willing to push myself to keep going. It was easier to accept the defeat and move on to something else.

Are you willing to put in the effort to go after what you want?

Are you willing to give it your all? Or are you going to give up at the first sign of defeat?

> *"Don't give up. If you give it your all and you push yourself you can get it done."*
> **— Sonya Parker**

I know it's hard. If it was easy, everyone would succeed at everything... but we don't. We give up along the way because we aren't willing to put in the maximum effort and keep pushing to success.

I wanted to step into my "Badassery" and unleash my inner Rocky, so I decided to learn the speedbag.

I was able to squeeze in 10 minutes of practice time each day after work. This wasn't much time at all, so I knew that if I wanted to succeed at this I was going to give it my all. I had to fully commit to making those 10 minutes each day count.

I first started out with the biggest speed bag I could find. I mean this thing looked like the size of a watermelon. I was pretty much guaranteed to hit it on every swing.

It was slow going at first but being able to focus solely on what I wanted to achieve, I was able to maximize my efforts and get the most out of each practice.

I was making progress. When I started out, I was punching one hand at a time. Eventually I became able to alternate my punching between each hand. After a few weeks I was able to down size the bag. My eye-hand coordination was getting better. My stamina was improving.

After a few months, all of the effort was really paying off. I had downsized the speedbag to what is known as a "peanut bag" which is crazy small.

Think about running on the treadmill. If you stop for a second, you will go flying off.

Using a peanut bag is similar but you are using your arms. Its bounce back is super-fast so one missed hit and it will break your rhythm.

> *"You've got three choices in life. Give up, give in, or give it your all."*
> **— Ritu Ghatourey**

Putting in the effort paid off. The speedbag is now a core staple of my workouts. I've even got my timing and coordination down so well that I can do it with my eyes closed. I would have never accomplished this if I hadn't put in the effort to keep going even when it seemed, at times, to be a losing battle.

Failure is a part of life. It's your ability to pick yourself up, dust yourself off, and continue to push yourself. Only then will you achieve what you want in life.

So I ask you again, are you willing to give it your all?

> *"Before success comes in any man's life, he's sure to meet with much temporary defeat and, perhaps some failures. When defeat overtakes a man, the easiest and the most logical thing to do is to quit. That's exactly what the majority of men do."*
> **— Napoleon Hill**

Most people view giving your all as starting out strong but immediately retreating at the first sign of defeat. They have a "I tried, I failed, I'm done," mentality. I view those defeats and failures as motivation to keep on going because eventually you will succeed.

> *"If you're not gonna go all the way, why go at all?"*
> — *Joe Namath*

Commit yourself to giving it your all. Get started:

- Start slow but make sure to start!
- Keep pushing ahead even when it seems like an uphill battle
- Commit to putting in all your effort and focus during the time you set aside. Don't half-ass it!

Avoid these common mistakes:

- Letting a temporary defeat stop you from continuing to push yourself
- Thinking you can accomplish something without putting in the effort. Rome wasn't built in a day

> *"The amount of effort you put in is the amount of results you end up with."*
> — *Catherine Pulsifer*

Take action right now. Make a commitment to yourself that you will put in 100 percent of effort. Have a friend or loved one hold you accountable to your commitment.

Face the Fear

Fear is defined as a distressing emotion aroused by impending danger, evil, pain, etc., whether the threat is real or imagined; the feeling or condition of being afraid.

If you knew for certain starting a new business would be a success, would you start it?

If you knew for certain asking that guy/girl out on a date, they would say yes, would you do it?

I bet the answer to both questions is YES.

Fear paralyzes us from moving ahead even when we know what we want and why we want it.

Is fear holding you back? What are you afraid of?

> *"The only thing we have to fear is fear itself."*
> — **Franklin D. Roosevelt**

Do you remember when I talked about my solo trip to Orlando earlier? It's the perfect example of facing fear head on.

The first night I was there, I went to the Cirque du Soleil show, La Nouba, located at Downtown Disney. I arrived to Orlando that afternoon. I thought that would be a good way to spend my first night there. It would be kind of a laid back night, nothing too crazy, right?

I had purchased my ticket a few weeks prior and I figured since this was not something I got to do that often I'd splurge for the better seating. After reviewing all of the available seats in the main section, the ticket price was the same for every row, so I bought my ticket in the front row.

Now, I don't know if you've ever been to a Cirque show but they have the tendency of pulling an audience member up on stage during the show.

As I arrived to the venue and found my seat, I silently told myself "I hope they don't pull me up on the stage." I don't know if fear was sitting next to me, behind me, or on my lap, but he fuckin' heard me!

The show begins and it progresses through the night, about halfway in I see those creepy looking clowns start coming to the edge of the stage. Talk about giving fear a physical identity.

I was like, "Uh oh, here we go."

Next thing I knew I'm being picked up and carried on the stage, now standing in front of hundreds of people and fear is standing there next to me, watching me, wetting his pants from laughter.

The creepy clowns then lay me down and all of these acrobats and BMX stunt guys begin jumping over me and around me. One BMXer came about an inch away from hitting my face with his tire…

And after it was over, I stood up, I took my bow, and received standing applause from the audience. I had a smile on my face the rest on that night. It was one of the best moments of my trip!

> *"He who has overcome his fears will truly be free."*
> **— Aristotle**

If I knew ahead of time I would have been pulled up on the stage, I probably wouldn't have gone to the show. The fear of standing in front of all those people with the spotlight solely on me would have kept me away.

But after experiencing that moment I couldn't figure out what I was so afraid of to begin with. I also realized you need to stare fear in the eyes and say "Fuck you! You can't hurt me! Get out of my way!" It's a hard thing to do, I know! Fear still gets the best of me from time to time, but when you can face your fears, you realize there wasn't anything to be afraid of in the first place.

Do not let your fears stop you from potentially missing out on what can be some of the best moments in your life!

> *"There is only one thing that makes a dream impossible to achieve: the fear of failure."*
> **— Paulo Coelho, The Alchemist**

Most people view fear as a reason to not do something. It keeps them stuck in their current state, no matter how bad the situation might be. I view it as something that will only make you stronger. As you start facing it head on, that creepy clown will turn into an adorable puppy.

> *"Do one thing every day that scares you."*
> — **Eleanor Roosevelt**

It's time to face your fears. Get started by:

- Leaning into your fear
- When facing fear, ask yourself what the worst possible outcome could be?
- Journal your past successes

Avoid these common mistakes:

- Using fear as an excuse as to why you can't accomplish something
- Making decisions or choices based on fear

> *"The man who fears losing has already lost."*
> — **George R.R. Martin**, *A Game of Thrones*

Take action right now by writing out the fears that are holding you back. Also write down why these fears are crippling you. What is it they endanger in you and in your life? What values and losses are you truly terrified of? What is it you want to protect?

Phase Four

The Sacrifice: Summary

It's time to take inventory of everything you've learned in Phase Four — The Sacrifice.

Build upon your Personal Discovery Statement by adding the following:

I am willing to sacrifice (insert your time wasters) to make the time needed to change my life. (Acknowledge here you are willing to make commitment to give it your all and add someone as your accountability partner). I will not let (insert your fears) stop me from achieving what I want.

Congratulations! You've made it through Phase Four.

Are you ready to move on?

Phase Five

The Process: Taking action

> "You don't have to be great to start, but you have to start to be great."
>
> **– Zig Ziglar**

You know who you are.

You know what you want.

You know why you want it.

You are willing to make the sacrifices and commit toward getting it.

But are you ready to take action?

In this phase, we will look at the ways to start taking action right now.

Responsibility

Responsibility is defined as the state or fact of being responsible, answerable, or accountable for something within one's power, control, or management.

Take action by taking responsibility.

Are you taking responsibility for your life?

Or are you playing the victim and blaming others?

> *"Man must cease attributing his problems to his environment, and learn again to exercise his will — his personal responsibility."*
> *— Albert Einstein*

The only person that can change or improve anything in your life is you.

Once you crush that victim mentality and take responsibility, you realize that it is you, and only you, that can take the action needed to get what you want, whether that is earning more money, learning a new skill, improving your confidence, finding a relationship, building a stronger body or losing body fat. No one else can do it for you. There may be people that help you along the way but it's ultimately up to you to make it happen.

An Olympic coach can only guide and train an athlete to be the best they can be. It's up to the athlete to win the medal.

Yes, not taking responsibility for your life is less demanding and less painful. You can just relax and blame your problems on someone else. But isn't why you are reading this right now because you want to change something in your life today?

This is one of the main reasons I wrote this book. Up until recently, I did not take responsibility for my life. I got trapped in that victim mentality where I thought:

- I can't save any money because I wasn't paid enough at my job.
- I can't learn a new skill or go back to school because I am too old.
- I can't get in better shape because I didn't have the right genetics.

> *"It is a painful thing to look at your own trouble and know that you yourself and no one else has made it."*
> **— Sophocles**

It wasn't until I chose to take responsibility for my life and stopped that bullshit "I'm the victim" mindset that I realized:

- I couldn't save money not because I wasn't getting paid enough but because I chose to pay for a cable TV package to get over 200 channels I didn't even watch or I bought another guitar when I hardly play the six guitars I already have.
- I couldn't learn a new skill not because of my age but because I was a lazy fuck that would rather lay on the couch and play mobile games for three hours straight rather than enroll in an online class or open up a book.
- I couldn't have six pack abs, not because of my genetics, but because I hated doing cardio. I didn't push my heart rate higher than a slow walk, and I didn't want a sweaty ass crack. I didn't want to eat a cleaner diet because, you know, it was that pizza holding a gun to my head telling me to eat it or else.

> *"If you could kick the person in the pants responsible for most of your trouble, you wouldn't sit for a month."*
> — ***Theodore Roosevelt***

Most people view the victim mentality a better alternative because it's easier and more comfortable, even though, ironically, they are unhappy. This leads to no action at all.

I view taking responsibility for your life the better path because it provides that extra boost that makes taking action easier. It allows you stop getting stuck in just thinking and wishing. You now have the power to do something about it.

> *"Action springs not from thought, but from a readiness for responsibility."*
> **— Dietrich Bonhoeffer**

In order to take responsibility for your life today, start with the following:

- Eliminate the blame and excuses
- Change those things within your control
- Understand you are the captain in command of this ship known as your life

Be sure to avoid these common mistakes:

- Not owning up to your mistakes and learning from them
- Not admitting you were causing negative or painful experiences for yourself

> *"If you own this story you get to write the ending."*
> **— Brené Brown**

Take action right now by listing any/all blame and excuses. List out what you can start changing today to take responsibility. It might help to simply write down everything that gives you that sinking feeling at first.

Then go through and ask yourself honestly what's within your power and what isn't. It's important to let go of the things you cannot change and to identify and purge the things you can.

But, I warn you, this will only work if you're honest with yourself. Don't be easy on yourself. Don't forgive yourself for things you can change. Don't lie to yourself. If you do, you can't make progress. If you truly love yourself, trust that admitting a mistake or fault will not cripple you. Now let's do this.

Be the Grasshopper

The term *"grasshopper"* originated from the Kung Fu television series from the 1970s, starring David Carradine as Shaolin priest Kwai Chang Caine. It refers to one who is a novice, a greenhorn, a student, or a subordinate.

Take action by learning and applying it to your life. Be the student.

Are you actively learning? Are you applying what you learn in your life?

> *"Education is not the filling of a pail, but the lighting of a fire."*
> **– W.B. Yeats**

Anywhere you can start learning something, do it and apply it.

When was the last time you read a book? (Other than this one, of course.)

Books are an inexpensive way to start learning and taking action. You can literally find a book on anything. If you can spend $10 on lunch, you can buy a book and, with a click of a button, you can have it instantly.

Do you want to learn how to cook, be a better lover, have more confidence, start an online business, lose weight, play chess, or become a ninja? There is most likely a book for that.

I consider myself a quick learner but I never used to read. I hated it. I found it boring and it would put me to sleep (blame and excuses). It wasn't until I recently started reading self-development books that I became hooked. I spend more time reading now than I did back in school and college. I just finished the book Daring Greatly by Brene Brown. I highly recommend checking it out!

> *"It isn't what the book costs. It's what it will cost you if you don't read it."*
> **— Jim Rohn**

Have you ever tried an online course?

Online education institutions and websites like Shaw Academy and Lynda.com, offer plenty of courses on a variety of topics and the fees are not that expensive. Cut back a little on going out to eat and drink every month and invest in yourself.

I have already taken a few courses from Shaw Academy and they have been great. The webinar lessons are live. If you can't attend the live classes, you can watch the recorded lessons at your convenience. That's what I typically do. I've just finished up their Introduction to Web Design course.

There are a variety of online options available to you.

> *"Self-education is, I firmly believe, the only kind of education there is."*
> **— Isaac Asimov**

What happens when your dog knows you are home from work or from being away for a while and he sees you enter the house? I remember when I was younger I had a Golden Retriever, Sugar. When I got home from school she basically turned in to a lunatic. She immediately ran over, jumping around with excitement and joy, licking me, barking, and probably wanting to go outside and drop one in the grass.

She wasn't thinking about how sad she was when I left her for all those hours. She wasn't worried that I had to go back to school again tomorrow. She was happy to see me right then, at that very moment.

You may have made mistakes in the past, you may have worries about the future, but learn to be in the present! It doesn't matter who you are, what you want, and why you want it. If you can't be in the present, you won't see all of the lessons that surround you each day.

> *"You learn something every day if you pay attention."*
> **— Ray LeBlond**

Most people view continuous learning into their adulthood as a burden, as a waste of time, and money. They spent all of those years in school and college, feeling like they never really learned anything. So why bother again?

I view continuous learning as a major ingredient for self-growth and success. As you continue to educate yourself and take action to apply it to your life, the knowledge you've learned takes a tangible form.

> *"Life is a continuous learning process. Each day presents an opportunity for learning."*
> **— Lailah Gifty Akita,** Think Great: Be Great!

Start taking action through learning by:

- Watching videos, reading books, taking courses, attending seminars
- Asking questions. The only dumb question is the question not asked
- Applying the knowledge you learn to your own life

Avoid these common mistakes:

- Thinking you are too old to learn something new
- Not applying what you learn

> *"Anyone who stops learning is old, whether at twenty or eighty."*
> **— Henry Ford**

Take action right now by listing out the methods by which you will start learning. Will that be in the form of books, classes, or seminars? There are all kinds of ways to grow in this life. The three forms I've noted down for you are just as valid as more unconventional ones. Wherever you are in life, it's always possible to grow. Knowledge is universal.

Learning in one area gives new perspective across other areas of your life. To truly embrace even one thing is to acknowledge everything. The world and the people that live in it are not as isolated as you may feel at times.

Everything is connected and learning will always provide new connections and opportunities. Acknowledging the gaps in your own knowledge and attempting to fill them is the path of wisdom.

That's why Socrates, the father of philosophy, always proudly spoke of knowing nothing. It's because acknowledging your own gaps is the first step in learning something.

Round up the Posse

Posse is defined as a body or force armed with legal authority; a group of friends or associates.

Take action by joining forces with people who have the same goals.

Do you have a posse of like-minded individuals who have your back and will push you to achieve what you want?

Do you have a group, community, or support system when the going gets tough?

> *"You are the average of the five people you spend the most time with."*
> **— Jim Rohn**

When you set out to achieve anything in life, it can be a lonely and discouraging road if you have no one there who supports your goal or dream. Being able to share your progress, victories, and even failures, with others who are also on the same path as you is critical to your success.

You can't waste your time with people who hold you back from achieving what you want with their negativity. So, it's vital you surround yourself with happy, successful, optimistic people. By doing this, you will become one of them.

You might think your family and friends will be there when you need support but that might not always be the case. Yes, your family and friends care about you but if they don't agree with what you are trying to achieve or do not see any value in it, they may try to pull you back into the negative whirlpool in the disguise of "we only want what is best for you" or "to keep you safe."

Their intentions may be done with love but that doesn't mean they are right.

Only you can decide what is best for you!

When I began my path of self-development, and my outlook on life started changing for the better, I received resistance from a few friends and family members that didn't really "get it". They didn't think the same way I did. It wasn't that they didn't care about me. They just couldn't understand or relate to why I was doing this. You see, when you get set in a certain way of thinking over many years, it becomes extremely hard to break that pattern.

You can share a different perspective with someone but if they are not willing to see it from your angle then they may never be open to accepting it.

> *"Share your ideas with people of like-mind and get motivated by their encouragements and experiences."*
> — *Israelmore Ayivor, Shaping the dream*

I started surrounding myself with people who had similar goals. Through social media and websites like MeetUp.com, I've been able to connect with some great people. I am now currently a member of a group where we meet once a week to discuss ideas, struggles, stories, etc. I've also joined private Facebook group communities of like-minded individuals through several online courses like, the Influence Academy program, at KnowledgeForMen.com. The group has been amazing. We constantly push each other to keep going, to go after what we want in life. I highly recommend checking out the website. It's one of the main inspirations for helping me write this book.

> *"You can do anything as long as you have the passion, the drive, the focus, and the support."*
> *— Sabrina Bryan*

Most people think that when they want to pursue a goal or make a life-changing move, they can do it alone. You can, but it will be a lot harder. Your tendency to quit will be greater when you don't have the right people supporting you.

I view having a group of similar people in your corner as a valuable asset in staying motivated, focused, and in pushing you to consistently take action and achieve your goals.

> *"A man's pride can be his downfall, and he needs to learn when to turn to others for support and guidance."*
> **— Bear Grylls**

Round up your posse. Get started by:

- Asking yourself if there are any friends or family you want involved?
- Check out local groups available in your area
- Find online communities that have similar interests

Avoid these common mistakes:

- Thinking you can do this alone
- Selecting group members that don't have the same commitment as you. The group is only as strong as the weakest link. Choose wisely

> *"Be strong, be fearless, be beautiful. And believe that anything is possible when you have the right people there to support you."*
> **— Misty Copeland**

Take action right now by deciding who you will round up to join your posse. Will that be in the form of friends, groups, an online community?

Move the Needle

P*rogress* is defined as movement toward a goal or to a further or higher stage.

So take action by making progress.

Are you consistently moving the needle? Are you making progress on a daily basis?

> *"I long to accomplish a great and noble task, but it is my chief duty to accomplish small tasks as if they were great and noble."*
> **— Helen Keller**

Whatever you want to achieve in your life, you have to remember that without consistent progress, you will never reach your goal.

Let's look at a task like grocery shopping. Yes, I know grocery shopping may not be a life-changing event but it will provide you with a better grasp of the concept. And it actually could be life changing, if your goal is improving your diet.

The Goal - Grocery Shopping

- Make a list = *Progress*
- Drive to the store = *Progress*
- Drive back home (you forgot your wallet) = *Pushed back*
- Drive back to the store = *Progress*

- Grab a cart = *Progress*
- Pick up everything on your list = *Progress*
- Run in to your neighbor = *Side-tracked*
- Check out at the register = *Progress*
- Pack up the car = *Progress*
- Head back to the cashier (you left a baggage behind) = *Pushed back*
- Drive home = *Progress*
- Unpack the car = *Progress*

End Result = Goal Achieved

Taking on any project or task, especially a new goal, can be overwhelming. Breaking it down and taking those small progress steps, no matter how miniscule they may seem, will eventually lead to your success. You will get side-tracked along the way. You will even get pushed back a few steps, but it's important to just keep moving forward.

> *"There are many ways of going forward, but only one way of standing still."*
> **— Franklin D. Roosevelt**

When I decided to create my own website, JourneyEvolution.com, I wasn't sure where to even begin.

I started getting overwhelmed thinking about everything I needed to accomplish, from choosing my domain name, to finding the right web host, to site creation, page content, etc.

I made the initial mistake of trying to tackle every aspect all at once. Instead of my website being this important goal I wanted to achieve, it became extremely stressful and a pain in the ass. I felt like Stretch Armstrong (probably one of the most ridiculous toys I had as a kid but still pretty fun). I was pulled in every direction. I was stretched out. I was not moving the needle at all. If anything, I was getting more frustrated and getting pushed back further.

If you know anyone that advocates multi-tasking everything, ask them how much do they actually get done and what's their blood pressure?

> *"Change is the parent of progress."*
> — **Steve Maraboli,** *Life, the Truth, and Being Free*

I realized the only way I was going to make my goal happen was to start breaking things down. I had to focus on one thing at a time. I had to make those small steps of progress. My website is still a work in progress but it would never be where it is today if I hadn't changed my strategy.

If I am able to take one step forward today, that is one more step further than yesterday. I see that as a win.

> *"Those who do not move, do not notice their chains."*
> **— Rosa Luxemburg**

Most people start a goal by tackling everything at once. This will most likely lead to one quitting. That's why so many people have a hard time finishing what they start.

I start a goal, or any project, by taking small steps of progress and consistently moving the needle, even if it is just a little each day. This will lead you to the path of success.

Move the needle. Get started by:

- Breaking down your goal in to pieces
- Focusing on one thing at a time
- Making small steps of progress consistently

Avoid these common mistakes:

- Allowing your goal to overwhelm you
- Getting discouraged if you get sidetracked or pushed back

> *"Without continual growth and progress, such words as improvement, achievement, and success have no meaning."*
> **— Benjamin Franklin**

Take action right now by listing out what you can do today to move the needle on a consistent basis. Remember, it can be about tiny steps. Small efforts.

Little victories. Anything that advances you, contributes to your life, even if it takes mere seconds.

Small as they are they're like seeds. Seeds being planted for a promised harvest. It can be comforting to look out over those tilled fields of your own life and imagine what will be.

Phase Five

The Process: Summary

It's time to take inventory of everything you've learned in Phase Five – The Process.

Add this last piece to your Personal Discovery Statement:

I am taking responsibility for my life right now by eliminating (insert your blames and excuses). I will start learning through (insert your learning methods) and begin applying it directly to my life. I will surround myself with a strong and solid support system by engaging (insert the names of your posse members). I am going to make consistent and steady progress by (insert your progress actions).

Congratulations! You've made it through Phase Five.

There is only one last question for you to answer.

Let's move on to see if you are ready.

Conclusion

The Palace

Imagine you are in a desert. The sun is beating down on you. It feels like it's getting hotter with every minute that goes by. Although you are hungry and tired, you still have water in your canteen.

As you look around, all that surrounds you is yellow sand.

Wait...

Far off in the distance you see a palace... It's magnificent!

You know you have only two options:

Option one: Start heading towards it, knowing the journey is going to be one of the toughest challenges you've ever faced in your life, but the reward will be worth it beyond compare.

Option two: Stay where you are, trying to survive for as long as you can on the little water you have left, before eventually perishing and becoming food for the vultures.

You are motivated and determined.

You hear your inner voice whisper to you:

"You know who you are."

"You know what you want."

"You know why you want it."

"You know what you are willing to sacrifice."

"And you are ready to take action."

You begin running towards the direction of the palace. You figure the faster you get there the better.

At first it's not so bad. You ask yourself jokingly, "How far can it be anyways?"

Your running, which seems like you've been doing now for days, turns into a walk. However, you have no intentions of giving up. You have no intentions of giving up because you have a goal. You know you are the only one who can reach your goal. You know what will happen if you stay where you are.

You are now starving, exhausted, and barely have any water left. You see the palace getting closer. You know you are on the right path but, by this point, you don't even know how much time has gone by. It could be weeks, months, or even longer.

Your inner voice, now getting louder, says:

"You know who you are."

"You know what you want."

"You know why you want it."

"You know what you are willing to sacrifice."

"And you are taking action."

As you continue, you fall to the ground. Exhaustion has taken its toll. You are out of water. The vultures are flying lower. You don't even need to look above you. You can feel them graze your head as they circle you.

You have so little energy left you have to crawl the rest of the way.

As you look behind you, you realize how far you've come… The palace is so close now and it's like nothing you've ever seen. The architecture is breathtaking. The golden domed towers reflect the bright sun, almost blinding you if you stare at them for too long.

You don't know how much longer it will take to get there but you must go on. You must go on because you are the only one who can reach your goal. You know what will happen if you stay where you are.

You want to reach that palace no matter what the cost.

Your inner voice shouts at you:

"You know who you are."

"You know what you want."

"You know why you want it."

"You know what you are willing to sacrifice."

"You are taking action."

What happens next?

Well. Only you can answer that.

Thank you!

Thank you for taking the time to read my book!

I hope this guide and process has helped you as it has for me.

I would appreciate your feedback and would love to hear what you thought about this book.

Please leave a helpful review on amazon so we can make a bigger impact for more men and women who need this book.

Please check out my website:

JourneyEvolution.com

You can also email me at:

Anthony@JourneyEvolution.com

Remember, you are not alone on this journey. Together we can become stronger individuals.

Educate. Engage. Evolve.

Thank you,

Anthony Butto

Founder of JourneyEvolution.com